NUESTRAS COMUNIDADES
—
AMERICAN COMMUNITIES

Vivimos en una granja

—

We Live on a Farm

Cody Keiser

Traducido por
Esther Sarfatti

PowerKiDS press™

New York

Published in 2016 by The Rosen Publishing Group, Inc.
29 East 21st Street, New York, NY 10010

First Edition

Editor: Katie Kawa
Book Design: Reann Nye
Traducido por: Esther Sarfatti

Photo Credits: Cover, pp. 3–24 (background texture) Evgeny Karandaev/Shutterstock.com; cover, pp. 9, 24 (barn) MaxyM/Shutterstock.com; p. 5 Mint Images - Bill Miles/Mint Images RF/Getty Images; p. 6 Steven Van Verre/ Shutterstock.com; p. 9 Casper Voogt/Shutterstock.com; pp. 10, 24 (crops) bjonesphotography/Shutterstock.com; pp. 13, 24 (tractor) B Brown/Shutterstock.com; p. 14 branislavpudar/Shutterstock.com; p. 17 (main) Christopher Elwell/Shutterstock.com; p. 17 (inset) Anastasiia Malinich/Shutterstock.com; p. 18 Dariusz Gora/ Shutterstock.com; p. 21 Chris Howey/Shutterstock.com; p. 22 holbox/Shutterstock.com.

Cataloging-in-Publication Data

Keiser, Cody.
We live on a farm = Vivimos en una granja / by Cody Keiser.
p. cm. — (American communities = Nuestras comunidades)
Parallel title: Nuestras comunidades.
In English and Spanish.
Includes index.
ISBN 978-1-5081-4735-0 (library binding)
1. Farm life — Juvenile literature. I. Keiser, Cody. II. Title.
S519.K45 2016
630—d23

Manufactured in the United States of America

CPSIA Compliance Information: Batch #BW16PK: For Further Information contact Rosen Publishing, New York, New York at 1-800-237-9932

Contenido
Contents

Vivimos en una granja grande.

We live on a big farm.

6

Una granja es una zona rural.
Eso significa que está en el
campo y no en una ciudad
o en un pueblo.

A farm is a rural area. This
means it's in the country
instead of a city or town.

Nuestra granja está rodeada de campo abierto. Las casas en nuestra comunidad están apartadas unas de otras.

There is a lot of open land around our farm. The houses in our community are far apart.

Sembramos plantas para comer y vender.
Se llaman **cultivos**.

We grow plants to eat and sell.
These are called **crops**.

Los granjeros utilizan muchas herramientas especiales. Los **tractores** sirven para tirar de las herramientas.

Farmers have many special tools. **Tractors** are used to pull these tools.

13

También criamos animales en nuestra granja. Las vacas viven en el **establo**.

We also raise animals on our farm. Cows live in the **barn**.

Obtenemos leche de las vacas que viven en nuestra granja.

We get milk from the cows that live on our farm.

Las vacas comen la hierba que crece alrededor de nuestra granja. ¡Comen mucha hierba!

The cows eat the grass around our farm. They eat a lot of grass!

A veces viene gente de la ciudad a visitar nuestra granja. Compran nuestras frutas y verduras.

People from the city sometimes visit our farm. They buy our fruits and vegetables.

21

¡La vida en la granja es muy atareada!

Life on a farm is very busy!

Palabras que debes aprender
Words to Know

(el) establo
barn

(los) cultivos
crops

(el) tractor
tractor

Índice / Index

Sitios de internet / Websites

Due to the changing nature of Internet links, PowerKids Press has developed an online list of websites related to the subject of this book. This site is updated regularly. Please use this link to access the list: www.powerkidslinks.com/acom/farm